101 Things I Learned in Psychology School

101 Things I Learned® in Psychology School

Tim Bono, PhD, with Matthew Frederick

CROWN
NEW YORK

Published in the United States by Crown, an imprint of Random House, a division of Penguin Random House LLC, New York.

CROWN and the Crown colophon are registered trademarks of Penguin Random House LLC.

101 Things I Learned is a registered trademark of Matthew Frederick.

Library of Congress Cataloging-in-Publication Data
Names: Bono, Tim, author. | Frederick, Matthew, author, illustrator.
Title: 101 things I learned in psychology school / by Tim Bono, PhD, with Matthew Frederick.
Other titles: One hundred one things I learned in psychology school
Description: First Crown edition. | New York: Crown, [2023] | Series: 101 things I learned | Includes index.
Identifiers: LCCN 2023011949 (print) | LCCN 2023011950 (ebook) | ISBN 9780451496751 (hardcover) |
    ISBN 9780451496768 (ebook)
Subjects: LCSH: Psychology.
Classification: LCC BF121.B58 2023 (print) | LCC BF121 (ebook) | DDC 150—dc23/eng/20230508
LC record available at https://lccn.loc.gov/2023011949
LC ebook record available at https://lccn.loc.gov/2023011950

Printed in China

crownpublishing.com

Illustrations by Matthew Frederick
Cover illustration by Matthew Frederick

9 8 7 6 5 4 3 2 1

First Crown Edition

From Tim

To Mom, Dad, Julie, Mike, Matt, and Christine—from whom I learned a lot about psychology long before I was ever in school . . . reverse psychology, anyway.

Acknowledgments

From Tim

Thanks to Christopher Lewis, Colin Keller, Kalen Furrer, Justin Lerner, James Compton, Linda Churchwell, Randy Larsen, Zvjezdana Prizmic-Larsen, and my students at Washington University in St. Louis.

From Matt

Thanks to Sorche Fairbank and Matt Inman, and a special note of appreciation to Marnie White.

101 Things I Learned in Psychology School

You need new skills to deal with your problem.

Cognitive behavioral therapy
- focuses on current thought patterns and behaviors
- develops new skills
- tends to be short-term

You need to look inside yourself to find the source of your problem.

Psychodynamic therapy
- oriented toward past events; assumes patient is stuck in a previous developmental phase
- seeks embedded patterns and hidden attitudes
- tends to be long-term

Talking cure

We'll start with 25 mg Zoloft and see how you do.

Psychiatry
- medical/scientific intervention
- necessary for biologically based mental disorders, such as schizophrenia
- may be deployed with psychological interventions

Medicinal cure

Three methods of mental health intervention

Psychiatry leans toward nature.
Psychology leans toward nurture.

Psychiatry generally holds mental illness to be the result of physical factors, such as faulty genetics or neurology, and favors a medical model for treatment. Psychiatrists, as medical doctors, typically prefer physical interventions, such as medication or electroconvulsive therapy.

Psychology tends to view mental illness as the product of environmental and biological factors. It most often seeks a "talking cure." Psychologists respect medicinal cures but realize they can be invalidating for some patients. Psychology believes people can really change. It is optimistic.

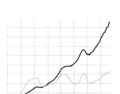

Scatter plot
shows all results
from a study

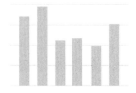

Bar graph (vertical)
effective for comparing
values among different
conditions or groups

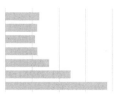

Bar graph (horizontal)
good for longitudinal
studies that track
changes over time

Line graph
effective for
demonstrating
change over time

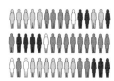

Pie chart
for discrete, mutually
exclusive categories that
add up to 100%

Pictogram
may suit lay audiences
but not effective for
robust data

Common data graphing formats

A psychologist is a statistician.

Behaviors, thoughts, and emotions are inherently amorphous, but questions about them must be made testable. A psychological study typically surveys or examines a sample group, and the resulting data is generalized to the larger population that the study group represents. For example, a survey of the sexual practices of a group of college students can be expected to inform on the sexual practices of college students in general. But study data can never be assumed to apply to a specific individual.

The type of question determines the type of research.

Longitudinal study: Collects data on the same people over time to learn how their behaviors change or develop. Time-intensive and usually expensive.

Cross-sectional study: Has similar goals to a longitudinal study, but compares individuals of different ages, e.g., 60-year-olds to 40-year-olds, at the same time.

Experimental study: Performed under controlled conditions with a variable that is measured and tabulated by assigning one intervention to one group and a different intervention to another. It is the only design that allows one to infer cause and effect.

Naturalistic study: Studies people "in the wild," ideally without their awareness. Lacks the control of a laboratory-based study, and therefore cannot identify, control, or measure all factors affecting behavior.

Correlational study: Measures two variables or behaviors separately to understand if they are related, such as income and happiness, or height and shoe size.

Case study: Examines the behaviors or characteristics of one individual, such as a person of extraordinary talents or a serial killer. In-depth and nuanced, but rarely used because it is not generalizable to others.

President-elect Harry Truman, 1948

A sample must represent those not in the sample.

A proper study sample is:

- **large enough to not be distorted by noise,** such as measurement errors, study subjects not understanding the question, or other random or idiosyncratic factors. But a sample should not be so large that erroneous or unusual data becomes common, thereby appearing to be a real effect. A typical minimum sample for a study is 40 people.

- **randomly selected from an appropriate population.** If the population from which the sample is selected is not representative, erroneous conclusions may be drawn. In a famous instance, a large headline in the *Chicago Tribune* incorrectly proclaimed victory for Republican Thomas Dewey over Democrat Harry Truman the morning after the 1948 presidential election. The conclusion was based on a poll of people selected randomly from the phone book. But at the time, Republicans were more likely than Democrats to own a phone.

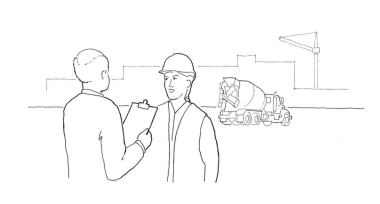

Seek concrete answers, not merely quantitative answers.

Many forms of research lead naturally to quantitative data. A study of happiness might measure the number of times someone smiles during an interaction, and a study of memory might measure the number of items an individual can recall after one, five, and ten minutes.

Asking people how many times in a year they are sad will also yield quantitative data, but it might not be reliable. Respondents' recollections may be inaccurate, and their definitions of "sad" could vary widely. But asking "How many times in the past year were you sad enough to call in sick to work?" prompts a concrete answer. Similarly, instead of asking people to rate how bad a procrastinator they are, perhaps ask, "How many of your utility bills are you currently late in paying, even though you can afford to pay them?"

Questions that seek concrete responses can help make abstract concepts clearer and ensure consistency from one study to the next.

□ completely agree

□ mostly agree

☑ somewhat agree

□ no opinion

□ somewhat disagree

□ mostly disagree

□ completely disagree

A 7-point scale is really a 5-point scale.

When surveyed, many people don't like to give extreme responses, such as "never" or "always." For this reason, a 7-point response scale is usually most effective, as it allows respondents to avoid extremes while keeping five clear options in play. Those without an opinion or judgment can select a midpoint, while those with mild or strong opinions can demonstrate their leanings without being absolute.

Surveys with an even number of response options usually should be avoided, as the lack of a midpoint forces respondents who would like to answer neutrally to indicate an inaccurate leaning.

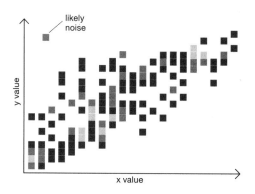

likely
noise

y value

x value

Scatter plot showing all results from a study

Subjectivity is more objective when you have a lot of it.

Much of what we want to know about people cannot be directly observed. Often, we have to ask people how they would respond to a given situation or how often they experience a particular emotion. Their answers, as in all surveys, will produce some noise: some respondents may be biased; some may deceive; and others may report inaccurately without realizing it. But the more people you survey, the more such responses tend to cancel one another out.

	– Decreases or removes something from the reward field	**+** Increases or adds something to the reward field
+ Seeks to increase or encourage a behavior	**Negative reinforcement**	**Positive reinforcement**
– Seeks to decrease or discourage a behavior	**Negative punishment**	**Positive punishment**

Positive isn't good. Negative isn't bad.

"Positive" and "negative" are value-neutral; they refer only to the direction of data. Positive indicates a presence or increase, while negative means an absence or decrease. A positive symptom of schizophrenia, for example, is hearing (adding) voices that are not there, while a negative symptom is an absence of normal emotional response.

It is incorrect to call punishment **negative reinforcement,** because both positive and negative reinforcement aim to increase a behavior, while punishment always seeks to decrease a behavior. A coach who makes a player run laps for being late to practice has instituted a **positive punishment.** If he bars the player from playing in a game, he has effected a **negative punishment.**

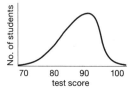

Negative skew

suggests test was
too easy

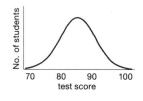

Normal curve

suggests test fairly
measured student abilities

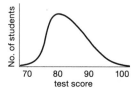

Positive skew

suggests test was
too difficult

Passing test grades in a college course

Most phenomena are bell-shaped.

Most human characteristics and behaviors, such as height, weight, intelligence, personality, reaction time, and work/play habits, follow a predictable pattern: the majority of data points fall among the middle values, while few are found at extremely high or low values. When graphed, this produces a symmetrical **bell curve.**

A bell curve can also be asymmetrical. For example, a graph of passing test scores in a college course may be **negatively skewed,** with a longer tail to the left. This may suggest that the test was too easy. A **positive skew** may indicate the test was too difficult or unfair.

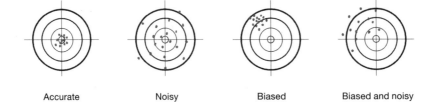

Accurate   Noisy   Biased   Biased and noisy

Where there are people, there is bias.
Where there is judgment, there is noise.

Bias exists when data consistently varies from the norm in a particular direction, such as when a speedometer always displays speeds that are 5% too high. A speedometer that gives widely variable readings is noisy—and maybe biased as well.

Bias and noise tend to cancel out in a large field. For example, a study of insurance premiums assigned by different underwriters for the same client revealed an average difference of 55%, indicating considerable bias and/or noise among individual underwriters. But for all policies across the entire company, the differences may even out, which would indicate no company-level bias despite considerable noise and bias within it.

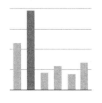

Mode

the value that
occurs most often

Median

half of occurrences
fall on each side

Year	Deaths
1979	541
1980	548
1981	354
1982	515
1983	497
Avg./year	491

Mean

the sum of values divided
by the number of values

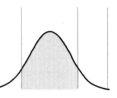

Interquartile range

omits 1/4 of results at
low and high ends

The mode, median, and mean are the same value when a bell curve is symmetrical.

What is most representative?

If the average test grade in a class is 84, we understand it as a **mean,** the result of adding up all the grades and dividing by the number of students. And we readily understand how any one student performed relative to it. But a mean is not always the most useful way of indicating an average. Imagine a small college whose students have a mean annual income of $10,000. If a typical student were replaced by Kylie Jenner, mean income might increase to $210,000—a mathematically accurate figure but, to most observers, unrepresentative. But both the **mode** and the **median** would remain close to $10,000 and would provide meaningful snapshots of student earnings.

The **interquartile range (IQR),** the middle 50% of a statistical distribution, can also be useful. In the above example, the IQR might show that the middle 50% of students make between $8,500 and $10,800.

Significant is not necessarily important.

Statistical significance means that the difference between two values in a test is large enough to register. A researcher must be able to identify significant data variations but should not assume that they are necessarily **important**. A finding is important when it has implications for the real world, such as new counseling techniques or medical interventions that improve the quality of life.

When study data shows a significant difference, identify specific ways it can help people in their everyday lives. If importance cannot be found, see if the data suggests new avenues and questions for research or practice.

wisdom — knowledge deeply contextualized in subjective experience

knowledge — contextualized information

information — contextualized data

data — uncontextualized facts

Data needs a story.

Research data is neutral information; a straightforward presentation of it is unlikely to mean much to those lacking a personal connection to it. The introduction of a narrative component into your presentation can enliven it and drive home its relevance to your audience and to the human condition.

Personal narrative: describes how the researcher became interested in the question that the study sought to answer.

Historical narrative: shows how the central question of the study has been explored by experts over the years, how changing contexts have altered it, and how the current study framed it.

Experimental narrative: tells the story of how the researcher created and organized the experiment, including methods, unexpected insights, failures, restarts, and ultimate successes.

Don't let your research be the end of the narrative. Circle your conclusions back to your starting point and suggest the course that the story may take in the future.

How to give a research talk

1   **Give it an accurate title.** If the topic is wonky, come up with something conversational, provocative, or punny, and add a subtitle that directly explains the topic.

2   **Present the elemental question or wondering that prompted your project.** A personal anecdote may help, but make sure it leads to a focused question that can be tested scientifically.

3   **Provide an overview of the existing research.** Identify gaps it has left that your research addresses.

4   **Begin presenting your own data no later than 15 minutes in.** An audience of fellow researchers or professionals will expect details, while a lay audience will be mostly interested in the application and meaning of your work.

5   **Direct your data toward a conclusion.** Show that you answered (or failed to answer) the scientific question posed at the outset. In either instance, acknowledge the limitations of your study and the gaps that remain.

6   **Allow time for questions and criticisms.** This is often the most valuable part of a talk—for the speaker as well as the attendees.

7   **Wrap up within an hour.** Provide takeaway resources for those interested in more information.

Put your unused ideas in the parking lot.

When developing a theory, follow the **Law of Parsimony:** pursue the most straightforward explanation that makes the fewest assumptions about what's involved in the phenomenon you are studying.

When writing up or presenting a study, anchor the entire presentation to one or two main arguments or theses. If you have too many ideas, the key ideas, even if they are good ones, will get lost and the entire presentation will be watered down. Either weed out the secondary ideas or develop a larger, unifying idea that collects all of them. Put your unused ideas in your "parking lot" and revisit them in a future paper or study—or accept that they may never be restarted.

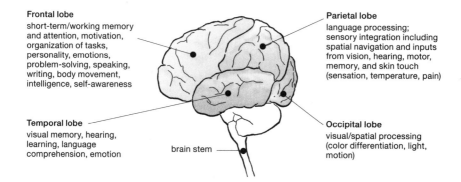

Frontal lobe
short-term/working memory
and attention, motivation,
organization of tasks,
personality, emotions,
problem-solving, speaking,
writing, body movement,
intelligence, self-awareness

Parietal lobe
language processing;
sensory integration including
spatial navigation and inputs
from vision, hearing, motor,
memory, and skin touch
(sensation, temperature, pain)

Temporal lobe
visual memory, hearing,
learning, language
comprehension, emotion

brain stem

Occipital lobe
visual/spatial processing
(color differentiation, light,
motion)

The four lobes of the cortex (outer layer of the brain)

Gray matter is pink.

The approximately 100,000,000,000 neurons that comprise the brain are mostly gray. However, most of the brain has a pinkish cast when observed directly, due to the blood coursing through its many vessels. Portions of the brain also appear red, white, and black.

Harvested, stored brains look gray-tan or gray-white due to preservatives, such as formaldehyde.

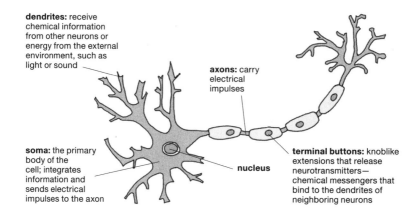

dendrites: receive chemical information from other neurons or energy from the external environment, such as light or sound

axons: carry electrical impulses

soma: the primary body of the cell; integrates information and sends electrical impulses to the axon

nucleus

terminal buttons: knoblike extensions that release neurotransmitters— chemical messengers that bind to the dendrites of neighboring neurons

Neuron components

The brain is electric.

Every aspect of thought, emotion, and behavior is attended to by communication among **neurons,** specialized cells that "fire" throughout our brain and body. These cells communicate via electrical impulses that send chemical messengers to other neurons. One set of neurons activates another, ultimately initiating thoughts, feelings, and behaviors.

The more a connection between neurotransmitters is repeated, the stronger and more permanent the relationship becomes, such that the activation of one neuron will lead to the activation of the other. If one repeatedly experiences pain after hearing a dentist's drill, for example, the neurons responding to the sound of the drill will activate the neurons that respond to pain, even when the pain itself is not experienced.

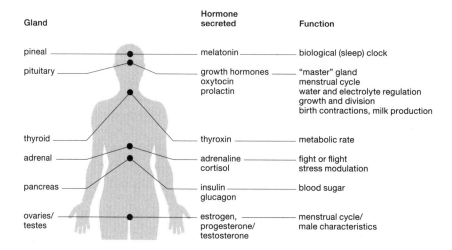

Gland

Hormone
secreted

Function

pineal ——————— melatonin ————— biological (sleep) clock

pituitary ——————— growth hormones ——— "master" gland
oxytocin   menstrual cycle
prolactin   water and electrolyte regulation
                             growth and division
                             birth contractions, milk production

thyroid ——————— thyroxin ————— metabolic rate

adrenal ——————— adrenaline ————— fight or flight
cortisol   stress modulation

pancreas ——————— insulin ————— blood sugar
glucagon

ovaries/ ——————— estrogen, ————— menstrual cycle/
testes   progesterone/   male characteristics
                       testosterone

Neurotransmitters are text messages. Hormones are snail mail.

Neurotransmitters and **hormones** are natural chemical messengers that affect our emotions, thoughts, and behaviors. The primary difference between them is how quickly they travel and, in turn, how long-lasting their effects are. Neurotransmitters travel very quickly (within nanoseconds) from one neuron to another, such as when they cause us to retract our hand quickly from a hot stove.

Hormones travel via the circulatory system; they take much longer to have an effect (from seconds to hours) and can be long-lasting. If you have an argument with someone in the morning and it is still affecting you late in the day, it is probably because the hormone cortisol was released and is continuing to circulate long after you thought you were over it.

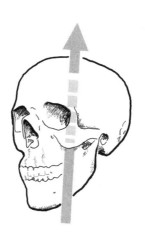

An extreme case illuminates the ordinary.

19

In 1848, construction worker Phineas Gage was directing a crew as it blasted rock for a railroad bed. An explosion propelled a 13-pound iron rod, 1¼" in diameter and 3"–7" long, into Gage's face. The rod passed upward behind his left eye, traveled through his brain, exited the top of his skull, and landed 80 feet away.

Gage survived the ordeal with no damage to his intelligence, memory, or basic functions such as eating, breathing, and maintaining body temperature. However, it was reported that the previously well-mannered, conscientious Gage became crude and moody. While subject to some dispute today, the reports that some aspects of Gage changed dramatically while others remained unchanged helped us consider that the brain has areas of specialized function. Previously, it was thought that the brain was a generalized blob, and that damage to one part would result in a decline in most or all aspects of behavior and function.

**No central brain
(cnidarians and others)**
nervous system consists
of reflex-based neurons
or neuron groupings
(ganglia located
throughout the body)

**Hindbrain
("lizard brain")**
baseline functions, e.g.,
awareness, reflex, eating,
procreating, fight or
flight, primitive emotions
(anger, fear, pleasure)

**Higher thinking
(humans)**
language; imagination and
abstract thought; reasoning
and critical analysis; reflection;
creativity, higher emotions;
meta-awareness (awareness of
one's awareness)

20

Higher thinking happens higher in the brain.

The areas of the brain that attend to basic life functions, such as breathing and heart rate, are located in its innermost layers. Areas that attend to more sophisticated functions, such as abstract reasoning, imagination, and critical analysis, are served by the brain's uppermost and outermost regions. This pattern of organization protects the parts of the brain most necessary for survival: if the outer layers are damaged, we will still be able to live.

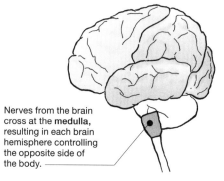

Nerves from the brain cross at the **medulla,** resulting in each brain hemisphere controlling the opposite side of the body.

The logical left brain/creative right brain distinction is a myth.

21

It is commonly and mistakenly thought that the left hemisphere of the brain is responsible for logical and analytical activities while the right brain handles creative and spatial tasks. This myth links to another: because each hemisphere in fact controls activity on the opposite side of the body, it is widely held that left-handers are inherently more creative than right-handers.

But there is no evidence that the brain has a logical-creative architecture or that any normal person uses one hemisphere more than the other. Different areas of the brain do attend to different functions, and greater activity is found at times in various sub-regions of the brain, but both sides of the brain are active in virtually all thoughts, emotions, and behaviors.

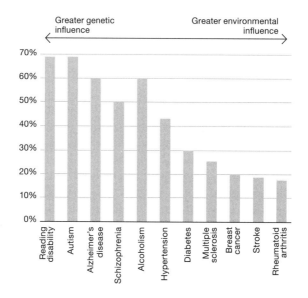

Greater genetic influence ← ⟶ Greater environmental influence

Percentage of identical twins sharing a trait
Source: Albert H.C. Wong, Irving I. Gottesman, and Arturas Petronis, "Phenotypic differences in genetically identical organisms: the epigenetic perspective." *Human Molecular Genetics,* 2005, Vol. 14, Review Issue 1

The womb isn't a neutral environment.

22

Cortisol, a hormone produced in the adrenal glands, helps regulate many critical aspects of the body, including metabolism, blood sugar, and sleep-wake cycles. It is also linked to stress: when you sense a threat, cortisol is elevated, curtailing some functions and redirecting energy to critical areas. After the alert has passed, cortisol levels return to normal.

Cortisol production ebbs and flows during pregnancy to accommodate fetal development. When a pregnant woman experiences physical or emotional trauma at inopportune times, cortisol may be inappropriately elevated, increasing the risk of miscarriage or otherwise harming the fetus. Studies suggest a more on-edge baby may result, with an increased likelihood of mental illness later in life.

Recent research indicates that genetic mutations naturally occur in the womb, even in the absence of trauma. While they affect a small percentage of an embryo's genetic makeup, they may lead to marked differences in eventual emotional and physical health.

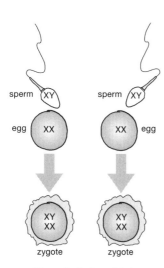

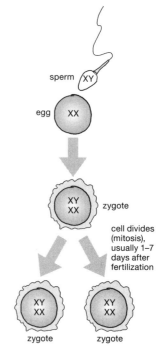

Dizygotic (fraternal) twins
50% genetic similarity at conception
49.9%± genetic similarity at birth

Monozygotic (identical) twins
100% genetic similarity at conception
99.9%± genetic similarity at birth

Twins raised apart are more similar than twins raised together.

23

Identical twins provide a nearly ideal control for studying the relative influences of nature and nurture. When twins are separated just after birth and reared in different families, there are strong indicators as to which psychological and behavioral outcomes are biological and which are environmental.

Interestingly, studies suggest that identical twins are more alike when reared apart than when raised together. It is thought that this is because the parents of intact twin sets encourage them to develop unique traits and interests (and the twins themselves may actively seek to differentiate themselves), while a twin raised apart from their identical other receives no such coaching. This leaves inborn traits to more strongly influence development.

0 to 18–24 months

Sensorimotor

sensory curiosity; coordi-
nation of motor response,
basic language skills; object permanence

18–24 months to
7+ years

Preoperational

egocentric; develops syn-
tax and grammar; uses
imagination and intuition,
struggles with logic and
abstraction

7 to 12 years

Concrete operational

more sociocentric; relates
abstract concepts to real
world; understands time,
space, quantity

11 years through adulthood

Formal operational

theoretical, complex,
abstract thinking and
reasoning; can plan,
strategize, and apply
concepts across contexts

Infants put things in their mouths. Toddlers put things in categories.

24

Babies are born with the capacity to use all five senses to explore the world. Sigmund Freud theorized, however, that infants in their first 18 months of life derive pleasure primarily from sucking or putting things into their mouths. Later, as they learn language, they begin to approach the world with **schemas,** or knowledge structures. If the four-legged creature in their home is a "dog," and the next-door neighbor has one too, "dog" may serve as their schema for the concept of a four-legged animal.

Over time, a child acquires experiences that do not perfectly fit into existing schemas. Upon learning, for example, the black-and-white-striped four-legged animal at the zoo is not a dog, a new schema, "zebra," may be born.

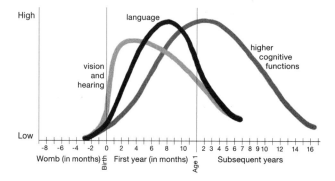

Synapse development

25

Progression may look like regression.

Children quickly learn language through imitation. A toddler, for example, might copy a parent by saying to his other parent, "Today we bought shoes for my feet."

A few months later, the same child might say, to his parents' dismay, "We buyed shoes for my foots." This doesn't mean the child has regressed in his English skills; in fact, he has advanced. He has learned that grammar has rules: nouns are pluralized by adding an "s," and verbs are made past tense by adding "ed." But he hasn't yet learned that some nouns and verbs are irregular.

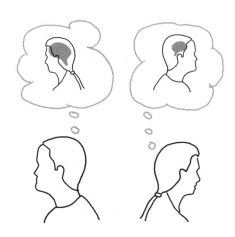

Theory of mind

26

In their first few years, children assume that their thoughts are common to every-one. This is why a toddler may cover her eyes with her hands and think she is invisible: she believes that others cannot see her because she cannot see them.

Eventually, children develop a **theory of mind,** by which they understand that others experience the world from different perspectives and know different things. This soon grows into a more abstract realization that others have different desires, motivations, and beliefs. As children mature further, they may be able to recognize in others things that others do not recognize in themselves: erroneous beliefs, ulterior motives, and buried emotions. They may also recognize the opportunity to lie, because they realize others do not have access to the same experiences and knowledge they have.

A properly developed theory of mind provides the basis for **empathy,** the ability to understand and share in the feelings of others. Individuals with schizo-phrenia and some other conditions often have an underdeveloped theory of mind.

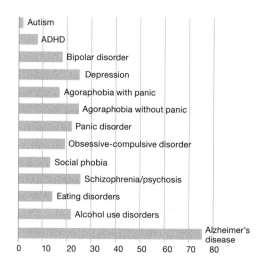

Approximate average age of onset

If you make it through your twenties, you are probably in the clear.

27

Most people who suffer from mental illness experience symptoms in their twenties, although a few disorders don't become evident or debilitating until much later. Compulsive hoarders, for example, usually do not seek help until at least their mid-thirties, despite often self-identifying the onset before thirty. Many report an onset before age ten; some as early as age four.

Psychologists are ethically limited in diagnosing patients under age eighteen. This is because a young person's psychology is in flux, and there is great danger in saddling a developing individual with a misdiagnosis.

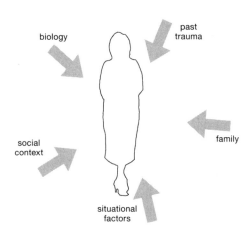

biology

past
trauma

social
context

family

situational
factors

Trauma can override innate personality.

Behavior in childhood predicts much about lifetime personality. An easily startled infant is likely to become an introverted or depressed adult. Children who are uncontrollable at three are more likely to become alcoholics. Four-year-olds who can resist a cookie for a later, larger reward are typically more disciplined as adults.

But extreme traumas, such as imprisonment, torture, war, sexual assault, abduction, and domestic violence, can override genetic determinants for personality. Trauma sufferers typically report chronic emptiness and hopelessness, hostile or distrustful attitudes toward the world, constant on-edgeness against threat, lifelong vulnerability to guilt and shame, and inclination toward self-injury. Those who do not experience prolonged emotional suffering may have traded it for physical suffering: in one study, Holocaust survivors who "felt as if the Holocaust was continuing" were more likely to experience mental disorders, while those who blocked the trauma from their memories had a higher mortality rate from physical illness.

The effects of an individual's trauma can be transgenerational, as those who endure it are often separated from their families and natural social networks. Their descendants may find a dearth of the emotional and practical support systems that benefit other individuals, resulting in continuing instability in their personalities.

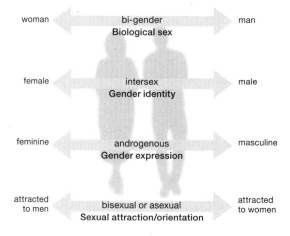

woman ← bi-gender / **Biological sex** → man

female ← intersex / **Gender identity** → male

feminine ← androgenous / **Gender expression** → masculine

attracted to men ← bisexual or asexual / **Sexual attraction/orientation** → attracted to women

Based on the work of Jennifer Bryan, Sebastian Mitchell Barr, and the Center for Gender Sanity

As nurture failed him

After a botched circumcision destroyed their infant son's penis, Ronald and Janet Reimer consulted John Money, an early expert in gender identity. Money believed that identity was shaped far more by nurture than genetics. As Bruce had an identical twin brother, Brian, he presented an ideal test case for Money's theory.

Money advised that the Reimers raise Bruce as a girl. Doctors subsequently removed Bruce's testes, fashioned a crude vulva, and administered hormones. Upon returning home, "Brenda" was outfitted with frilly dresses and made to play with dolls. During annual visits to Money, Brenda and Brian were forced to simulate heterosexual intercourse with each other. Money publicly reported the case a success when the twins were seven. But Brenda's behaviors remained stereotypically masculine. He beat up Brian and urinated while standing, leading his peers to call him "cavewoman."

At 14, Brenda threatened to kill himself if made to visit Money again. His parents then told him the truth. Brenda subsequently received a double mastectomy, testosterone injections, and two phalloplasty operations, and became "David." He later married a woman, but his efforts at normalcy were undermined by depression, rage, and underemployment. Meanwhile, Brian was diagnosed with schizophrenia and died from a drug overdose at 36. Two years later, David, after his wife's request for a separation, took his own life.

29

"Trauma in a person, decontextualized over time, looks like personality. Trauma in a family, decontextualized over time, looks like family traits. Trauma in a people, decontextualized over time, looks like culture."

—RESMAA MENAKEM, psychotherapist

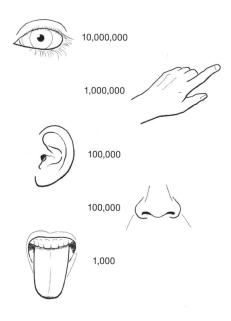

30

Approximate transmission rates of the senses in bits per second

Emotions link body and intellect.

Early psychologists held emotion to be a cognitive awareness of the body having reacted to an event. If an external source presented a threat, for example, one would experience sweating, a pounding heart, and heavy breathing, and would then feel fearful.

But because different emotions may accompany the same physiological characteristics, physical symptoms alone cannot be responsible for emotions. Sexual attraction, for example, shares physical symptoms with fear, such as increased heart rate and sweating. This suggests that one's existing cognitive framework is also in play. In fact, emotions and their physical characteristics can arise in the reverse order and even without external stimuli. Thoughts about a loved one, for example, may lead to worrying about their absence, which may lead to fear that something has happened to them, which may lead to an increased heart rate.

The mind's interplay with physiology can lead to misattribution of our emotions. In one study, men whose heart rate increased from crossing a rickety bridge found a female research assistant more attractive than men who interacted with her on solid ground in a calm state. Researchers believed that the men mistook their fear for sexual arousal.

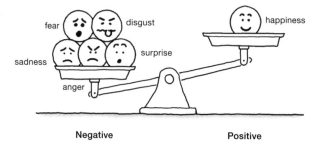

The six basic emotions

Emotions are asymmetrical.

32

There are more ways to feel distress than to feel good. Painful events last longer and carry more psychological weight than happy events, even when they are equal in magnitude. Studies have shown, for example, that for most people the pain of losing $50 is greater than the joy of gaining $50.

This tendency is tied to our cave-dwelling past: our distant ancestors needed to be more vigilant to dangers that threatened their survival than to "happy" events. This asymmetry helps explain today why we may quickly adapt to the thrill of a higher-paying job, but ruminate endlessly over a minor dispute with a co-worker.

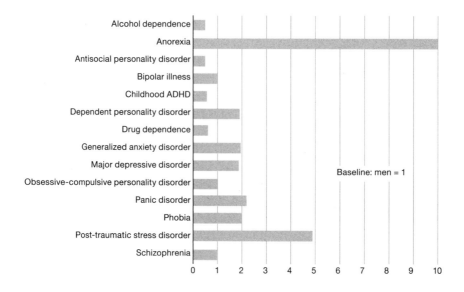

Frequency of disorders in women compared to men

33

Men and women are equally emotional.

Women are more likely than men to turn their distress inward in the form of anxiety or depression. For men, distress is more likely to be directed outward through aggression and other problems with impulse control.

Extroverts are less responsive.

Extroverts may seem full of energy and highly engaged in what's going on around them. But, counterintuitively, the brain of an extrovert is less reactive to external stimuli than the brain of an introvert.

34

The difference between extroverts and introverts is detectable from birth, although not always in the way one might expect. In studies, some infants react mildly to environmental stimuli, such as a mobile hung over their crib, while others respond animatedly. But the quieter babies tend to grow into extroverts while the more active babies tend to become more introverted. Researchers theorize that quiet babies are not impressed by a mild stimulus; they need higher levels of stimulation to feel engaged. As adults, they seek out active environments. Babies that react strongly to a mild stimulus may find it agitating; as adults they seek out quieter environments where they won't experience distraction and discomfort.

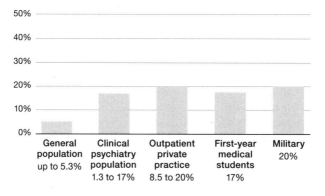

Estimated prevalence of narcissistic personality disorder
Source: Elsa Ronningstam, PhD, "Narcissistic Personality Disorder: Facing DSM-V," *Psychiatric Annals,* March 2009

Male: narcissistic ≈ female: histrionic

Narcissists and **histrionics** are attention seekers. Narcissists are selfish, have an inflated sense of importance, and lack concern for others, although at the outset of a relationship they may act subserviently or empathetically to attract another person. Histrionics seek attention by being theatrical—superficially emotional, dramatic, flowery, giggly, flirtatious, or flighty.

In many ways, narcissism caricatures stereotypical male behavior while histrionic personality disorder (HPD) exaggerates female behavior. However, both disorders are found in men and women. Almost 75% of those diagnosed with narcissistic personality disorder are male, while HPD occurs about equally among men and women.

Do you think
men are funnier
than women?

Yeah, when
they're naked.

Men are "funny."

Studies show that most people judge men to be funnier than women: we tend to rate a given joke funnier when attributed to a male author than to a female author. This may be an instance of the **halo effect,** by which one makes an initial positive assumption of a person (or gender), which leads to attributing additional positive characteristics to them, even if undeserved.

Hey, if they can put a
man on the moon, why
not all of them? Ha ha!

You're
hysterical.

Women are "hysterical."

Hysteria comes from the Greek *hysterika,* meaning "uterus" or "womb." In ancient Greece, male doctors thought that defects in the womb caused excessive anxiety, fainting, insomnia, sexual aggression, and displays of emotion.

These notions persisted for centuries. In the Victorian era, doctors administered pelvic massage to women to induce orgasm and "restore" their mental health. In the 1880s, Dr. J. Mortimer Granville invented the mechanical vibrator, which liberated male doctors from their arduous labor. His invention, powered by a large generator, was limited to installation in doctors' offices. Over time the device was refined and miniaturized, and it eventually found its way into private homes.

By the 20th century, "hysteria" lost its association with its uterine roots and became a descriptor for any person in an extended state of uncontrolled emotion. But the American Psychiatric Association did not remove hysteria neurosis from its *Diagnostic and Statistical Manual of Mental Disorders* until 1980.

Bottling
tamping down negative
feelings in the hope of
maintaining an even keel

Venting
letting negative feelings "fly,"
with the ostensible goal of
purging them from the self

Emotional disclosure
thoughtfully processing
feelings to gain a more
rational perspective

Venting makes us angrier.

When angry, we may want to scream or throw something, thinking it's best to "let it out." If we later feel better, we may attribute our restored mood to having vented. But studies show that venting tends to further increase anger and delay our return to emotional baseline. And when we eventually do calm down, we have the same, or even more, work to do as we would have had before venting.

"Allowing our anger to fester creates the perfect environment for anger to turn into hate, and that is not okay. The best thing we can do is be honest about how we are feeling."

39

—NEDRA TAWWAB, mental health therapist

Age	Core dilemma/crisis	Ideal virtue
0–1½	trust vs. mistrust	hope
1½–3	autonomy vs. shame	will
3–5	initiative vs. guilt	purpose
5–12	industry vs. inferiority	competency
12–18	identity vs. role confusion	fidelity
18–40	intimacy vs. isolation	love
40–65	generativity vs. stagnation	care
65+	ego integrity vs. despair	wisdom

Erik Erikson's life stages

The central task of adulthood is integrity.

In early adulthood, the main challenge we face is differentiating ourselves from our family of origin. As we proceed farther, decisions about lifestyle, career, and family become part of the permanent scheme of adulthood: we work, attend to our loved ones, and contribute to our community.

In late adulthood, the primary struggle comes from reflection on one's life choices. Psychologist Erik Erikson defined this struggle as integrity versus despair. Those who fear that their choices were poor (for example, pursuing material success over family and social connectedness) are likely to feel despair. Those who believe their lives have been spent well are likely to experience old age with a sense of well-being and satisfaction.

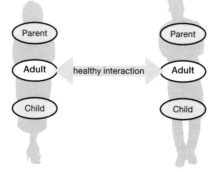

healthy interaction

Parent

Adult

Child

Parent

Adult

Child

After the Transactional Analysis model by Eric Berne, M.D.

Be an adult.

Adults ideally conduct themselves *as* adults. They act rationally, genuinely, and respectfully; address other adults as peers; and resolve differences constructively and empathetically. But when in conflict, we can easily slip into an unhealthy Parent-Child mode that caricatures an ordinary parent-child relationship. The Parent is powerful, knowing, domineering, bullying, and condescending; the Child is vulnerable, unknowing, insecure, and subordinate. Communication becomes hierarchical rather than peer to peer, and manipulative rather than fair and rational.

41

A person who condescends through the **Parent mode** usually expects the other party to respond in the **Child mode.** A person who feels victimized by another may slip into Child mode, blame the other for their situation, and demand that they fix it, thereby designating the offending party the Parent. Sometimes, both parties act as Parent and treat the other as Child; this tends to lead to a frustrated standoff.

In a proper **Adult mode,** we do not victimize or act as victim. We do not instill fear in or blame the other for our circumstances. We don't set verbal traps or issue hidden messages. We accept the other person's perspective and respond with compassion. We are secure enough to acknowledge our shortcomings and those parts of the conflict for which we are responsible.

sociopathic/psychopathic   neurotic

too self-directed   too other-directed

Too much responsibility or not enough?

Neurotic individuals tend to take too much responsibility for their actions. They repeatedly question their past actions and wonder if they could have done something differently to achieve a more satisfactory outcome. In contemplating future actions, their fear of a wrong decision can lead to "paralysis by analysis." However, neurotics, because of their tendency to be overly responsible, are more inclined to enter into a therapeutic relationship with a psychologist.

Character-disordered individuals tend to take too little responsibility for their actions. They can be rash, impulsive, and unempathetic. They are not inclined to introspection and almost never seek therapy. Narcissists, psychopaths, and sociopaths are examples of character-disordered individuals.

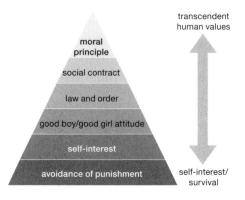

42

Based on Kohlberg's stages of moral development (1958)

A moral person values law and order. A very moral person might not.

Lawrence Kohlberg built a model of moral development on Jean Piaget's child development model. As individuals mature, Kohlberg postulated, they pass through increasingly sophisticated stages by which they negotiate moral dilemmas and distinguish right from wrong.

The lower stages are experienced mostly in childhood and are oriented toward learning social rules, avoiding punishment, and fitting in. Most adults advance to Stage 4, where they look to the formal laws of society to resolve moral issues. At higher levels, one pursues a morality that answers to humanity's universal needs and aspirations, which may be at odds with societal norms.

43

Guilt is productive. Shame is wasteful.

Guilt is feeling bad about something you have done. Guilt stemming from your bad actions tells you that you are inherently good—that you know right from wrong. It may lead you to console those you have hurt, repair damage you have done, or atone in other appropriate ways.

Shame is feeling bad about who you are. It tends not to drive efforts to repair, but to lead one to avert their gaze, retreat into the self, and reach out less. An accumulation of guilt, left unaddressed, becomes shame: we do something wrong and feel guilty about it, but ignore it; we do something else wrong, and ignore it; eventually we feel bad not only about our misdeeds but about ourselves.

44

How to apologize

1   **Don't just do something; stand there.** Don't rush into saying "I'm sorry"; this is not the essential task. Instead, listen carefully to understand how the person has been hurt. Don't explain your actions or intentions or make counter-accusations.

2   **Say "I'm sorry for what I did," and mean it.** Apologize for your actions and for their impact on the other person. Don't give an "apology-lite" by saying, "I'm sorry, but . . ." or "I'm sorry if you were hurt."

45

3   **Make things whole.** Hold yourself accountable for your actions and the resulting harm, and identify specific steps to set things right. It's important to ask the victim if there is anything you should do, but it's also important to take the initiative to fix things rather than act only according to the victim's requests.

4   **Never again.** If your behavior doesn't change, an apology is meaningless. Create a plan to prevent the hurtful actions from happening again. Use the opportunity to make your relationship stronger.

With thanks to Molly Howes

Stimulus
from external
source

Sensory storage
brain very briefly
retains initial
sensory impression

Short-term memory
can hold 7+ pieces
of information after
cessation of stimulus

No rehearsal
memory is
discarded/
forgotten

Retrieval/recall
may be permanent

Long-term memory
can hold an infinite
amount of information

Rehearsal
memory is revisited
or reinforced

You forgot the name of the person you just met because you didn't rehearse it.

Most people can mentally retain between five and nine pieces of new information. But if the new information is not used or repeated, it is soon lost. Rehearsal trains the mind to recognize new information as important and to store it in long-term memory, increasing the likelihood of recall. It is theorized that people knocked unconscious in an accident often do not remember the event because they were denied an opportunity to mentally rehearse it.

46

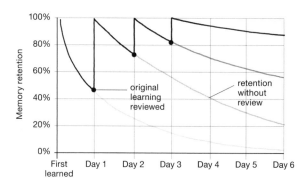

Ebbinghaus's forgetting curve

Interruption aids memory.

Repeated experiences, such as a baby hearing its mother's voice, tell the brain that something is important to remember. But a surprising contributor to memory retention is interruption. Psychologists Bluma Zeigarnik and Kurt Lewin found that waiters have excellent memories of customers' orders if not yet paid; afterward, they quickly forget them. Lewin theorized that an uncompleted task establishes a "cognitive tension" that improves access to memory. Once the task is completed, the tension is relieved and the unneeded memories are discarded.

This may also explain why a student who successfully "crams" for a test tends to forget more afterward than other students, and why students who interrupt their studies to engage in unrelated activities remember material better than those who do not take a break [McKinney 1935; Zeigarnik 1927].

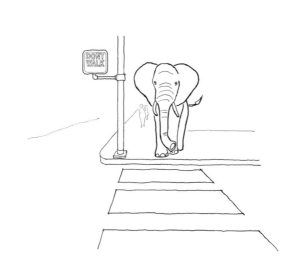

47

Forgetting makes the mind more efficient.

Some researchers argue that the purpose of memory is misunderstood: it does not exist to transmit information with high fidelity over time. Rather, its purpose is to promote intelligent, long-term decision-making. Our imperfect recollection of past experiences aids this goal: if our memories were perfect and precise, we would find it very difficult to generalize learnings from old experiences to new situations. For example, we may remember almost being hit by a car years ago but forget many details. This allows us to carry forward the most important learning: look both ways twice before crossing the street.

An overly detailed memory can result in rigid or debilitating thought patterns that limit adaptation and growth, as observed in individuals suffering from post-traumatic stress disorder.

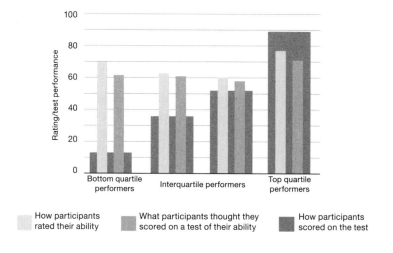

48

Self-perception of skills versus real-world performance
Source: J. Kruger, and D. Dunning, "Unskilled and unaware of it: How difficulties in recognizing one's own incompetence lead to inflated self-assessments," *Journal of Personality and Social Psychology* 77, no. 6 (1999): *1121–34*

People who aren't smart can't tell.

Most people have a fairly realistic view of how good they are at tangible skills, such as knitting, playing pool, or dribbling a basketball. But when it comes to skills of a more abstract or intellectual nature, such as problem analysis and logical reasoning, we are often poor estimators of our abilities. Highly skilled individuals tend to underrate themselves, while the low-skilled tend to over-estimate. In the case of the latter, this is because the skills people need to be good at something are the same skills they need to discern that they *aren't* good at it.

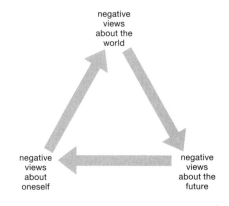

49

Beck's cognitive triad (or the negative triad)

Depressed people are realistic.

Early theorists posited that depressed people had an inaccurately negative view of themselves. More recent research has found that they tend to evaluate their shortcomings fairly accurately. Research also suggests that the opposite is true with happy people: they tend to think they are better than they are.

UK psychologist Richard Bentall proposed that happiness be designated a "major affective disorder, pleasant type." He argued that happiness meets most of the criteria for a mental disorder: it is statistically abnormal, is evidenced by a discrete cluster of symptoms and cognitive abnormalities, and likely involves abnormal functioning of the central nervous system. Bentall anticipated the counter-argument—that happiness cannot be deemed a disorder because it is not negatively valued. His preemptory response was that it is unscientific to dismiss an argument on a value basis, because science must be value-neutral.

Bentall did not really believe that happiness is a mental illness; rather, he wanted to show that it is impossible to define and diagnose a mental disorder without making a value judgment.

50

"To be stupid, selfish, and have good health are three requirements for happiness, though if stupidity is lacking, all is lost."

—GUSTAVE FLAUBERT

51

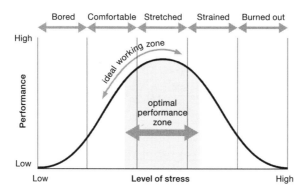

Some anxiety is good.

Anxiety is normal and even useful. It can warn us of danger or motivate us to get things done. Our performance in fact tends to increase when we are a little anxious. But if we are too anxious about a task, we may lose focus and perform poorly.

An individual who experiences frequent, intense, and extended anxiety may have a disorder. Those who do not experience anxiety may also have a disorder: while this could indicate a calm, confident disposition, it may symptomize demotivation or depression. A person who never experiences anxiety might be emotionally insensitive and prone to excessive risk-taking.

52

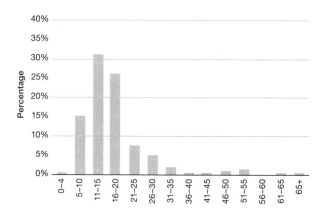

At what age did you first experience performance anxiety?
Source: 2015 Musician's Health Survey by composeddocumentary.com

Perform difficult tasks in isolation and easy tasks in front of others.

Tasks within one's skill range are generally enhanced as anxiety increases: students will hunker down and work more efficiently on a paper as a deadline approaches, a singer may belt out high notes with greater quality in front of an audience, and athletes can complete heroic plays during a high-stakes tournament game when an enthusiastic crowd cheers them on.

Tasks outside one's skill range tend to be diminished as anxiety increases. An impending deadline will diminish the quality of a paper if a student does not understand the material he is writing about; an actor's performance will be worse if she has not studied her lines; and an athlete will be less likely to make a critical play if it calls for a move he is unfamiliar with.

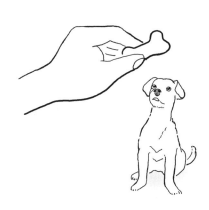

53

How to train a pet

Use behavior capturing. Reward and build on a behavior that the animal already exhibits. For example, if you notice that your dog is about to sneeze, command "Sneeze!" Reward the dog immediately. Eventually, the dog may sneeze on command.

Start small and build. Complex behaviors can be taught by rewarding simpler acts, then rewarding incrementally more complex behaviors that are closer to the desired outcome.

54

Don't reward every time. If you reward a behavior only sometimes, an animal won't become completely accustomed to receiving a reward in response to the behavior and will be more likely to perform it in the absence of a reward.

Continue occasional rewards after the animal has mastered a behavior. A dog may lose motivation in the long run if it is never rewarded for a behavior. Occasional rewards and signs of approval will help your pet maintain an association between the behavior and the positive outcome.

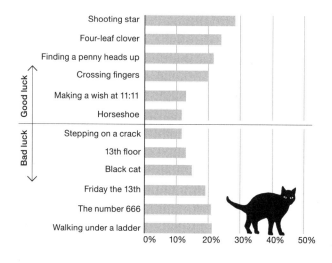

Percentage of respondents holding superstition
Source: YouGovAmerica poll of 1,000 Americans, April 26–30, 2022

Superstition results from inadvertent reinforcement.

When something good or bad happens, we might associate it with unrelated things happening at the same time. A student who aces an exam might attribute it to wearing a blue T-shirt, then wear the shirt for all future exams. A baseball player who tapped the plate three times before getting a hit may believe it made him a better hitter. Such associations are the result of **illusory correlation,** the erroneous belief that separate events are related. We often base such generalizations on a single case.

The behaviorist B. F. Skinner argued that pigeons behave in a way that is analogous to human superstition. He gave them food at regularly timed intervals. If food happened to be administered right after a pigeon cooed or tilted its head, the pigeon would coo or tilt again to receive more food, even though the behavior and the feeding were unrelated.

55

Magnitude
size of reward

Valence
importance of reward

Expectancy
likelihood of attainment

Components of extrinsic motivation

Rewards can backfire.

Offering someone an **extrinsic** reward, such as payment or ice cream, for performing an activity they inherently enjoy can undermine their **intrinsic** motivation. Instead of continuing to derive pleasure from the process (e.g., practicing the piano or doing well in school) or its end product (mastery of a skill), they may decrease their effort and shift their attention to the reward that awaits.

Similarly, or perhaps oppositely, punishment sometimes increases a behavior it is meant to curtail. In one study, some parents were late to pick up their children from a daycare center. The center introduced a late fee to deter tardiness, after which even more parents were late in picking up their children. The center, by creating a policy for lateness, had inadvertently handed parents an excuse for it: lateness was justified by a payment.

56

Satisficers

- make good-enough decisions
- don't obsess over options
- move on after deciding
- are more satisfied with outcomes

Maximizers

- try to make perfect decisions
- exhaustively consider options
- second-guess themselves
- are more likely to regret decisions

The more options, the more disappointment.

Most people facing a decision can keep track of about seven options. When more options are added to a choice field, we tend to become confused and frustrated. An extremely large number of options can be especially anxiety-producing, as it may lead us to believe that one of the choices before us is perfect. Fear of picking a wrong option may outweigh the potential delight of selecting an excellent or even good enough one. After we have made our decision, the first hint of disappointment in it may lead us to imagine that a different choice would have led to greater satisfaction.

"If people go through life looking for good enough results, the choice problem will take care of itself. Go through your day getting a good enough cup of coffee and a good enough toasted bagel and so on and so on and life will look much sunnier."

—BARRY SCHWARTZ, psychologist

McKayla Maroney
Silver medalist, vault, 2012 Summer Olympics

Bronze beats silver.

Our happiness in the aftermath of a competition is shaped not only by our performance, but by how close it was to a better or worse outcome. Studies of the facial expressions of Olympic medalists have found that third-place winners tend to exhibit more happiness than second-place winners. While the silver medalist may be haunted by the fraction of a second that kept him from winning gold, the bronze medalist can imagine the fraction of a second that might have sent him home without a medal at all.

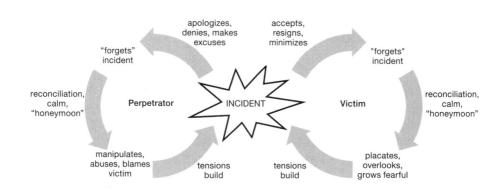

59

The abuse cycle

Abusers find people who don't weed out.

Victims of abuse do not ask for or deserve abuse. But adults who were abused as children can inadvertently enable further abuse. They may overlook slights, putdowns, or manipulations from a new friend, partner, or co-worker because the echoes of childhood seem familiar and normal. This may open a door to more egregious misbehaviors by the abuser. Similarly, abusers tend to view their own behaviors as normal or justifiable, and to seek out people who are more accepting of them.

Adults who did not experience abuse as children appear more likely to weed out abusers—not necessarily because they recognize them as such, but because they find them irrelevant, uninteresting, and annoying.

60

Dude, you gotta
lose the model!
Reality isn't binary;
it's shades of gray!

Isn't it binary to say
that a model has to
be perfect, or you
can't use it at all?

Satisficers

Maximizers

We understand reality better when we leave parts of it out.

An ordinary road map isn't reality; it's a *model* of reality. It is useful because it is selective and imperfect: if a map accurately represented every aspect of a landscape, it would be of little value in helping one traverse it.

Language is likewise a model; it captures reality imperfectly. "Blue" does not perfectly convey the color of a given blue object, which will unavoidably be lighter or darker or have more green or red in it than the blue in one's mind. But this does not diminish the value of "blue" as a model; without such imperfect descriptors, how would we describe anything?

When know-it-alls dismiss a model for its shortcomings, it may be because they misunderstand the point of a model. They may think that the person advancing the model is arguing that the model is reality, when it is merely a lens for viewing it. And they might not understand that acceptance of a model does not require one to devalue or negate all other models. A blue object can also be long, heavy, smooth, and slightly greenish. Each imperfect model brings us closer to understanding the whole in ways that we could not attain if we sought only models that are perfect and complete.

61

Replicability

Can the study be
repeated by others with
the same result?

Validity

Did the study measure
what it was intended to
measure?

The cause might be the effect.

When we smile, the **zygomatic muscles** draw up the corners of the mouth. These muscles are easily exercised at will, allowing us to "fake smile"—to show we are pleased when we really are not. A truer, **Duchenne smile** results from genuine happiness. It invokes the involuntary contraction of the **orbicularis oculi,** the muscles around the eyes.

In a classic study, researchers analyzed the college yearbook smiles of 141 women, and followed them for 30 years. Those who had exhibited Duchenne smiles tended to live longer, have fewer divorces, and exhibit greater overall well-being than students with less intense or forced smiles. A separate study of player photos on baseball cards reached similar conclusions.

More recent research has found that some individuals can voluntarily activate the orbicularis oculi, calling into question long-accepted understandings of the Duchenne smile. Further, it is inconclusive whether the students and ballplayers were more successful in life because of their easy smiles, or if their lives were already better than those of their peers at the time of the photographs. This would have made them more likely to smile genuinely at the time, and perhaps given them a head start toward success in life.

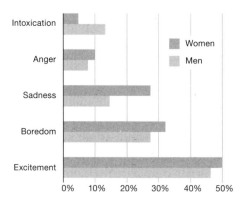

62

Impulse shoppers' states of mind
Source: Survey of 1,000 U.S. adults in December 2014 by Creditcards.com

Put space and time between expense and experience.

Shelling out cash for a product or service activates the same brain regions that are activated by the anticipation of pain. For this reason, businesses often create distance between the pain of payment and the reward of receiving. For example, theme parks and vacation destinations often offer promotions and discounts for paying in advance. By the time the experience is engaged, the discomfort of spending money has subsided, leaving more room for enjoyment. Ironically, this may increase the likelihood that people will spend more money during the experience on upgrades, souvenirs, and snacks.

63

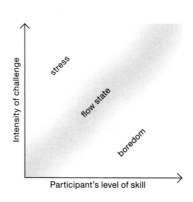

Time is malleable.

Albert Einstein showed that time passes at different rates depending on distance from a center of gravity and speed of travel. This difference is too small to notice in everyday experience, but it directly affects the Global Positioning System (GPS). An orbiting GPS satellite, being farther from the earth's center of gravity than the earth's surface is, must move faster than the earth's surface to maintain a constant position relative to it. Consequently, a satellite clock runs about 38 millionths of a second slower per day than an earthbound clock. This discrepancy is continuously corrected by the GPS system to avoid errors at user level.

Even though time passes at the same rate for us earthbound humans, our perception of it can vary. **Flow experiences** occur when one is so deeply engrossed in an activity that the perception of time is altered. For example, many great football running backs and basketball players report that the game slows down when they are performing at their peak. An artist or craftsperson engrossed in producing a new work may think that minutes have gone by rather than the hours shown on the clock, or may work so fluidly as to accomplish hours of work in far less time.

When one has more work to do than seems doable in the time available, stress can be eased by doing a good deed for someone else. This leaves one with objectively less time, but it can create a new sense of time abundance that boosts one's confidence and motivation to complete critical tasks in time.

64

"Time is relative; its only worth depends upon what we do as it is passing."

—ALBERT EINSTEIN

65

Meditation doesn't clear the mind; it focuses the mind.

Meditation dwells closely on a single task or concept, such as paying attention to one's breathing. When distracting thoughts arise during meditation, one recognizes and acknowledges them, then non-judgmentally directs one's attention back to the matter of focus.

By practicing the redirecting of obtrusive thoughts, we become better at identifying and managing what is and is not useful in everyday life, leading to greater productivity and personal well-being.

66

States not allowing an insanity defense

Insanity is a legal, not psychological, term.

A psychologist never diagnoses a patient as insane, and the word does not appear in the American Psychiatric Association's *Diagnostic and Statistical Manual of Mental Disorders*. Insanity is a concept used by courts of law to help distinguish guilt from innocence. It describes a defendant who cannot distinguish right from wrong or fantasy from reality, or who cannot function normally due to psychosis or a lack of impulse control.

67

Negative symptoms
- difficulty initiating plans, speaking, expressing emotion
- disordered thinking and speech
- difficulty with logic
- deficits in attention and memory

Positive symptoms
- hallucinations, hearing voices
- paranoid delusions
- exaggerated or distorted perceptions
- abnormal behaviors or movements

less responsive
to medication

more responsive
to medication

Schizophrenia isn't multiple personality disorder.

People suffering from schizophrenia struggle to distinguish between real and unreal experiences. Research suggests that this difficulty is the result of defects in **sensory gating** mechanisms, which help normal individuals screen out peripheral stimuli and focus on a core task. Whereas most people can easily ignore blinking lights or nearby conversations at a cocktail party, a schizophrenic may feel bombarded by them. This may explain the common symptom of hearing voices: a healthy person recognizes "inner voices" as one's own thoughts, but the schizophrenic might struggle to differentiate them from countless other stimuli, creating confusion as to their source.

68

Serotonin
stabilizes moods, feelings of
well-being, and happiness; aids
in sleeping, eating, digestion

Dopamine
pleasure; plays
motivational role in
brain's reward system

Endorphins
diminish the perception of pain,
act as sedatives, aid relaxation;
produce "runner's high"

Oxytocin
bonding, love, trust; also
controls key aspects of
female reproductive system

Drugs are impersonators.

Prozac, Ritalin, and similar drugs work because of their similarity to chemicals that the brain naturally produces. The brain's receptors for Prozac and Ritalin are designed by nature to receive serotonin and dopamine.

69

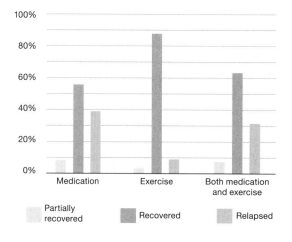

Clinical status 10 months after initiation of treatment for depression
Source: *Psychosomatic Medicine: Journal of Biobehavioral Medicine*

Exercise beats Zoloft.

In 2000, Duke physician Michael Babyak enrolled clinically depressed patients in a study. Some were prescribed Zoloft, an anti-depressant; a second group was prescribed exercise; and a third group received both prescriptions. Within four months, those who only exercised were as likely to have recovered from their depression as those who had taken the psychiatric drug. Six months later, the exercisers were doing even better than the Zoloft takers.

The groups developed markedly different perspectives on their treatment. Although all were following a prescription, those who improved through the drug regimen tended to view their improvement, and presumably their depression, to have been caused by factors outside their control. But the exercisers were inclined to view their improvement as resulting from an internal source— themselves. Zoloft helped the patients; exercise empowered them.

70

THE CAT

We read a wrod as a whole, not eahc letter by itslef.

Our minds do not discern individual pieces of information separately, but look for larger patterns. When the mind receives imperfect information, it naturally fills in gaps or makes corrections so that it aligns with prior experiences, existing knowledge structures, and situational expectations, to make a whole. The mind operates as if interpreting a pointillist painting, in which an image is detected by understanding how the dots collectively form an image, instead of trying to make sense of each dot individually.

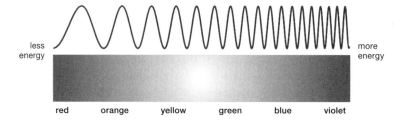

71

Visible light spectrum

An object's color is the opposite of what we see.

When light strikes an object, some light waves are absorbed by it while others bounce off. A red object absorbs all colors but red, and sends the red wavelengths back to our eyes. A black object absorbs effectively all wavelengths of light and reflects none, while a white object absorbs almost none and reflects nearly all. We assign a color to an object based on the wavelengths it rejects rather than the wavelengths it retains.

72

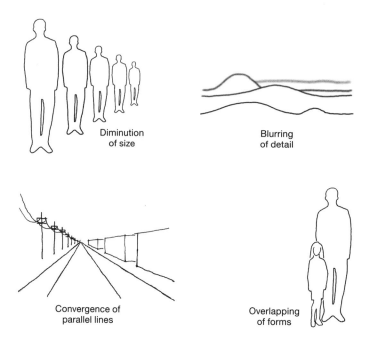

Diminution
of size

Blurring
of detail

Convergence of
parallel lines

Overlapping
of forms

Some perceptual depth cues

The brain sees more than the eye sees.

When light enters the eye, it creates an image on the retina, a light-sensitive tissue at the back of the eyeball. The brain combines this image with other information—from one's other eye, from the physical context, and from existing mental models—to infer three-dimensional space.

The brain even fills in an inherent blind spot in the eye caused by an absence of receptors where the optic nerve exits the retina.

73

How to find your blind spot

1   Place the graphic on the left-hand page directly in front of you, with your nose centered between the cross and the circle.

2   Close your left eye and stare at the cross with your right eye while maintaining awareness of the circle in your peripheral vision.

3   Slowly move the page closer or farther away, while focusing on the cross.

4   When the circle disappears, it is located in your blind spot, where the optic nerve interrupts your retina.

74

That conspiracy
theory was disproved!

That's what they
want you to think.

We resolve dissonance by changing whatever is easiest to change.

Cognitive dissonance: the mental discomfort that results from holding beliefs, values, or attitudes that are inherently contradictory. Often, we relieve our discomfort by "explaining away" the discrepancy rather than by resolving it honestly.

Cognitive bias: an error in reasoning resulting from limited awareness or information.

Barnum effect: the tendency to accept vague information, such as telepathic readings or horoscopes, as true even when meaningless.

Confirmation bias: the tendency to overlook contradictory new evidence or interpret it in favorable ways in order to confirm one's prior beliefs or theories.

Hindsight bias: a belief that one could have predicted or prevented an event that has already occurred, in the manner of the "Monday morning quarterback."

Actor-observer bias: the tendency to explain others' behaviors as a function of their personality ("The guy who cut me off is a jerk!") and our own behaviors as due to external circumstances ("Others are depending on me to not be late").

Self-serving bias: an exception to the actor-observer bias in which one attributes their own successes to personal characteristics or initiative ("I studied really hard") and failures to external circumstances ("The test was unfair").

75

Reference line

A B C

Comparison lines

The Asch conformity experiments

Psychologist Solomon Asch showed groups of students a card with a line on it, then another card with three lines. He asked them to identify the line on the second card that matched the length of the line on the first card.

In each group, only one student was an actual subject; the others were actors whom Asch had coached to give a particular answer. Asch found that when one or two actors gave a deliberately wrong answer while others gave the correct answer, it had little impact on the subject's responses. But three or more wrong actors increased the conformity of the subject markedly. When all actors gave the same wrong answer, subjects agreed with it about one-third of the time.

When asked why they went along with the wrong answers, most study subjects said they wanted to avoid ridicule. It is believed that this desire is even stronger in ordinary life, where right and wrong answers are often far less evident. Conformity pressure further increases when we are around people with higher social status and when a task becomes more difficult; our insecurity or uncertainty motivates us to turn to others for insight.

"You become the average of the five people you spend the most time with."

—JIM ROHN, author and motivational speaker

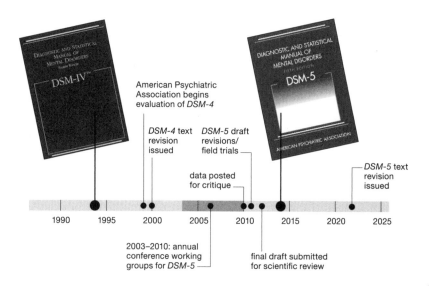

American Psychiatric
Association begins
evaluation of *DSM-4*

DSM-4 text
revision
issued

DSM-5 draft
revisions/
field trials

data posted
for critique

DSM-5 text
revision
issued

1990   1995   2000   2005   2010   2015   2020   2025

2003–2010: annual
conference working
groups for *DSM-5*

final draft submitted
for scientific review

Drafting, publication, and revision of the *Diagnostic and Statistical Manual of Mental Disorders*

New information is old.

It takes about 17 years for published research to become accepted practice. Writing a new psychology textbook takes several years, which means that classroom instruction may be more than two decades behind the times.

A 2017 study found that most psychology textbooks include landmark psychology studies that have been significantly revised or even debunked. For example, many textbooks cite the 1964 murder of Kitty Genovese in Queens, New York, as an example of the **bystander effect,** which theorizes that people are less likely to help a victim when other people are present. Dozens of neighbors were said to have witnessed the attack on Genovese without intervening or calling the police. But such accounts were shown decades later to have been sensationalized by local newspapers.

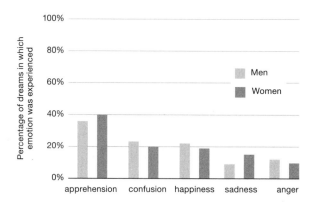

78

Emotions reported to have been experienced during dreaming
Source: Calvin Hall and Robert Van de Castle via Five Thirty-eight

It's hard to study dreams.

Scientists know very little about the function or meaning of dreams. Sigmund Freud suggested that they tap into repressed desires and conflicts, although there is no scientific evidence that unresolved childhood issues lead to being chased through a car wash by Abraham Lincoln.

Psychologist Calvin Hall Jr. sought to empiricize the study of dreams. He collected 50,000 dream reports, in which he found similar patterns among people around the world, although the frequency of specific dream elements varied widely. He believed that his findings indicated a relationship between our dreams and our waking concerns and interests.

Neuroscientist Allan Hobson argued that dreams are the result of random brain pulses, which initiate accidental narratives; these narratives become subsequently meaningful as the mind relates them to non-dream thoughts and emotions.

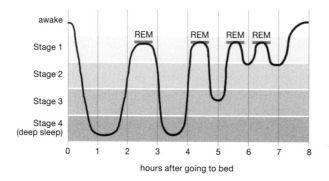

Typical eight-hour sleep cycle

Nap for less than 20 minutes or more than 90 minutes.

When we sleep, our brains cycle between fast-wave activity (light sleep) and slow-wave activity (deep sleep). In the first 20 minutes we are in fast-wave sleep, making it easier to wake up because our brain activity is not far from that of our awake state. But as brain waves slow down more, it becomes difficult to wake up without feeling groggy. After about 90 minutes, the brain cycles back to fast-wave sleep, making it easier to awaken feeling refreshed.

80

Fear, avoidance   Decreasing fear   Seeking exposure   Fondness

Robert Zajonc's mere exposure effect/familiarity principle

Familiarity doesn't always breed contempt.

The more an organism is exposed to an unfamiliar stimulus, assuming the stimulus does not present a threat, the greater liking the organism will gradually show toward it. The initially fearful organism may even come to actively seek the stimulus and react fondly to it. The **mere exposure effect** lies at the heart of most advertising: the more we see a product, the more likely we are to purchase it.

The reverse is true for stimuli that are unpleasant, dangerous, or irritating: repeated exposures usually amplify the initial negative feelings. However, carefully controlled exposures to fear-inducing stimuli can reduce or eliminate **phobias,** which are largely unjustified or irrational fears. If the feared stimulus is introduced in small doses (such as having a person with a fear of heights step up one rung of a ladder), the fear may be small enough to manage. Over time, the fear over the modest step will dissipate and the person can fully face the previously feared stimulus.

81

Read the middle at the end.

It's best not to read an academic research paper in the order in which it is presented on the page. Instead, read the introduction and then the end discussion to gain context for the more complex, detailed middle sections.

The major sections of an academic paper are:

1   **Introduction:** presents a review of the previous research on the general topic of the paper. The end identifies a question or questions that previous research has not answered, setting the stage for the current study.

2   **Methods:** describes the techniques the study used to measure the topic being studied.

3   **Results:** presents the study data, typically in tables and charts, and a narrative explanation and summary.

4   **Discussion:** reminds the reader of the question or questions the paper sought to address, the major findings, and the directions future research should take.

82

How to teach

1 **Prepare, but not too much.** Organize the content in the order you expect to present it, but don't be rigid. Put the least important material in the middle. If you run short on time, this is the material to skip.

2 **Start before you start.** As students enter, ask them about themselves. Make a mental note of things they bring up that you can refer to during class.

3 **Begin at the end.** Start your lecture with the message you want the students to leave the class with.

4 **Be interactive.** Ask questions after each major set of ideas. Use clicker technology to gauge student understandings in real time before moving on.

5 **Allow students to shape the direction of the class.** Trust yourself to follow tangents that arise and still hit your planned crescendo near the end.

6 **Save the most important material for the end.** However your class goes, preserve at least 10 minutes to cover your ending material so you are not rushed.

83

7 **Remain a student.** We teach most effectively when we are trying to answer questions for ourselves. Design your lecture to explore questions that matter to you. Link your material to recent research and current events.

Consequences of
Erudite Vernacular
Utilized Irrespective
of Necessity:
Problems with Using
Long Words Needlessly

Daniel M. Oppenheimer

Bigger words suggest smaller intellect.

Psychology professor Daniel M. Oppenheimer studied how our word choices affect how others perceive our intelligence. He replaced long words in various essays with shorter words and asked study participants to evaluate the "author." The participants consistently judged the version with shorter words as the product of a more intelligent person, associating it with positive personal qualities such as capability, confidence, and likability.

In carrying his study to other venues, Oppenheimer found that corporate stocks with hard-to-pronounce names were less likely to be purchased. Business leaders who used long words prompted frustration and confusion among employees, who often ignored complex vocabulary in new policies and directives. Oppenheimer has even argued that politicians with hard-to-pronounce names are disadvantaged in elections.

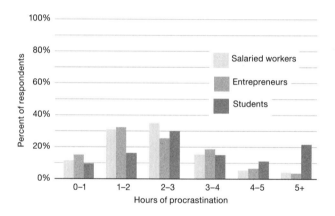

How many hours did you procrastinate yesterday?
Source: Survey of 2,219 people by Darius Foroux, dariusforoux.com

Little problems, unaddressed, become big problems.

Life requires us to solve problems—get the car tuned up, have a difficult discussion with the boss, make compromises with loved ones. But it is easy to deny or put off dealing with a problem. We leave it to fester, hoping it will go away. When it doesn't, we feel worse about the problem, and worse still about our procrastination. Our anxiety deepens and creeps into other areas of our lives, where we are ignoring other problems. We become irritable, ashamed, and depressed, and flash anger at things we aren't angry about. We come to carry a shapeless, overwhelming burden through our waking hours, the precise source of which has become impossible to identify.

One can suffer legitimately by solving life's little problems as they arise, or face much harder-to-solve problems further down the road.

85

"In life, we can't always control the first arrow. However, the second arrow is our reaction to the first. The second arrow is optional."

—THE BUDDHA

86

Projection
attributing a feeling one has about a
person to that person

Transference
redirecting a feeling one has about a third
party onto a more immediate person

Therapy is an alliance.

Most patients want to connect with their therapist. They want to be liked and understood, to participate in diagnosing their problem, and to actively implement a solution.

As a therapist, stay on the client's side of their problem. Use your relationship not only to gain insight into the problem, but to develop sympathy for how they view and engage with the world. If you sense overly enthusiastic disclosure, inappropriate attachment, disinterest, or veiled hostility, you have probably opened a window into the client's other relationships.

Tune in to changes in your relationship with the client over time. If a client expresses dissatisfaction with the course of the therapeutic alliance, it may be because a breakthrough is imminent: the client may sense a confrontation of his defenses or the crumbling of a long-held belief system, and project the cause of his discomfort onto the therapist.

87

Detective Frank Columbo, television character created by Richard Levinson and William Link

Feign innocent confusion at the patient's discrepancies.

If a patient doesn't act according to a promise or describes events in a way that contradicts an earlier account, don't tell the patient they lied or fell short. Instead, without referencing the previous discussion, ask innocently, "Why did you do that?" or "How did that turn out?"

88

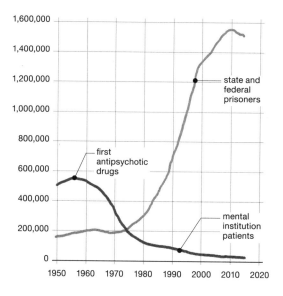

U.S. prisoners and mental health inmates
Sources: The Sentencing Project and U.S. Department of Health and Human Services

The Rosenhan Experiment

In 1973, psychologist David Rosenhan reported that he and 11 colleagues had presented themselves to 12 psychiatric institutions, where they pretended to hear voices. All were admitted, after which they acted normally and told staff they no longer had symptoms. The pseudo-patients were held for as long as 52 days and an average of 19 days; all but one were diagnosed with schizophrenia. Staff interpreted their normal behaviors as symptoms, for example, characterizing their note-taking (for purposes of the experiment) as pathological. Meanwhile, in three of the institutions, 35 of 118 legitimate patients expressed suspicions that the pseudo-patients were impostors. When the pseudo-patients were eventually released, it was on condition that they admit to being mentally ill and agree to take antipsychotic drugs.

A hospital subsequently challenged Rosenhan to send pseudo-patients to its facility to test its screening abilities, which it believed robust. Rosenhan agreed. The hospital labeled 41 of 193 new patients as Rosenhan-sent impostors, and another 42 as suspected impostors. Rosenhan said that he had sent none.

In 2019, author Susannah Cahalan investigated the Rosenhan experiment and reported that it was largely faked.

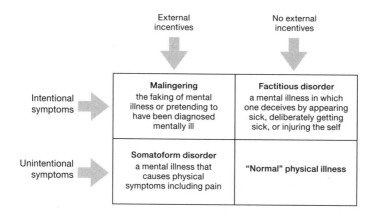

	External incentives	No external incentives
Intentional symptoms	**Malingering** the faking of mental illness or pretending to have been diagnosed mentally ill	**Factitious disorder** a mental illness in which one deceives by appearing sick, deliberately getting sick, or injuring the self
Unintentional symptoms	**Somatoform disorder** a mental illness that causes physical symptoms including pain	"Normal" physical illness

Adapted from B. Adetunji, et al, "Detection and management of malingering in a clinical setting," *Primary Psychiatry,* Vol. 13, No. 1, 2006

Faking mental illness is evidence of mental illness.

Malingering is the faking of psychological symptoms or pretending to have been diagnosed with a mental illness in order to gain an external reward. For example, one might fake a mental disorder to get away with a crime, gain disability benefits, get time off work, or attract attention from family members. Malingering tends to abuse the medical system, as it can divert attention and resources from genuinely needy patients.

Malingering indicates that a psychological problem nonetheless exists. Psychologists have developed techniques to identify malingering, such as tests that a malingerer "fails" by agreeing to a doctor's suggestion of symptoms that cannot exist.

"It's a lot harder to convince people you're sane than it is to convince them you're crazy."

—JON RONSON, author, quoting a psychiatric patient

Historical
deemed deviant in
a specific era

Situational
deemed deviant in some
contexts but not others

Cross-cultural
deemed deviant in more
than one culture

Categories of deviant behavior

Societies decide abnormality.

The traits and behaviors of only a small percentage of people fall outside societal norms. But norms are neither universal nor necessarily fair. They marginalize some behaviors or modes of engagement that may be valued in other societies. An especially curious, impulsive child, for example, may have been esteemed on the pre-civilization frontier, where seeking new experiences and forging into the unknown was a necessary aspect of life. But modern societies, in requiring children to sit still in a classroom seven hours per day for the better part of twelve years, will perhaps unavoidably diagnose some of them with attention deficit hyperactivity disorder.

Where's
Mary today?

She called in with
cancer. She should be
better by tomorrow.

Mentally ill, mentally diseased, or mentally injured?

A stomach bug or winter cold is technically a disease, but ordinarily we use *disease* to describe a serious pathology that threatens an individual's overall well-being and survival. We most often describe someone with a condition that is expected to pass relatively uneventfully as *sick* or *ill*. And we use *injury* to label a localized harm from an external source.

The mental health field does not distinguish between disease, illness, and injury; does this contribute to the stigmatization of mental illness? If "mental illness" describes deeply intractable pathologies, is it an appropriate label for temporary anxiety? Can we have true empathy for persons suffering from a biologically rooted psychosis if our nomenclature equates their condition with a passing bug? Is it fair to label adults who suffer emotionally from abuse endured in childhood as mentally ill when the source of their suffering is an injury by an external actor?

brain

a physical, objective entity; a vessel for electrical impulses that attend to perception, thought, behavior, etc.

Mind

a subjective entity; debated if it resides in the brain or throughout/ beyond the body; relates to holistic awareness, self-awareness, and felt knowledge

Szasz: There is no mental illness; there are only problems in living.

Psychiatrist Thomas Szasz believed it wrong to classify those suffering from mental problems as diseased. Disease, he noted, is rooted in a physical fault, but the mind—one's mental center—is a conceptual rather than physical entity. The term "mental illness," he argued, should be understood as a metaphor. "Minds can be 'sick,'" he wrote, "only in the sense that jokes are 'sick' or economies are 'sick.'" Psychological problems are properly recognized as deviations from social norms or "problems in living," not as illnesses. In medicalizing such problems, we sidestep important questions of society and morality.

Szasz further argued that when we identify a biological basis for a mental illness—for example, tracing "madness" to syphilis—we prove his point that an apparent psychopathology is actually a physical pathology. And if we were to show that all of the mental conditions we now call mental illness are actually physical diseases, there would be no need at all for the concept of mental illness.

restlessness

hives, itching,
or rash

joint or
muscle pain

suicidal
thoughts

chills or
fever

Common side effects of Prozac

Nature doesn't draw boundaries where we draw them.

When a psychiatric intervention is prescribed to a patient, it cannot be focused solely on the diagnosed condition. For example, a gene, hormone, or enzyme identified as the cause of depression and targeted for treatment might also help a person be introspective, competitive, or creative; sense danger or dishonesty; think long-range; or feel empathy. Treatment of a patient's wayward quality will likely alter other aspects of him or her.

95

| **Hard sciences** | **Soft sciences** |
| non-human phenomena | humans and human systems |

Hard sciences

- seek to be value-neutral
- often builds investigations on laboratory isolation
- can establish reliable cause-effect relationships
- relies on quantitative factors
- conclusions from formal study usually apply to individual cases

Examples: physics, chemistry, biology, geology, astronomy, mathematics

Soft sciences

- cannot be value-neutral
- laboratory isolation of factors is usually impossible
- difficult or impossible to establish direct cause-effect relationships
- many qualitative and unknown factors
- formal study conclusions cannot be presumed to apply to individual cases

Examples: psychology, political science, economics, sociology

The soft sciences are hard.

The factors that shape human behavior are largely amorphous and likely infinite. This makes it very difficult to frame questions about people in scientific terms, identify reliable variables and controls for a study, and draw clear conclusions from the data. Consequently, new studies frequently contradict earlier studies, and certainties accumulate very slowly. Even when a clear principle of human behavior can be determined, its applicability can be presumed only of people in general; it cannot be presumed to apply to a specific individual. Treatment of a patient must nonetheless be based in a deep awareness of the scientific literature. But intelligent intuition is also called for to interpret and address the patient's unique situation. Psychology research is a science. Psychology practice is an art, deeply informed by science.

96

"Science is often misrepresented as 'the body of knowledge acquired by performing replicated controlled experiments in the laboratory.' Actually, science is something broader: the acquisition of reliable knowledge about the world."

—JARED DIAMOND

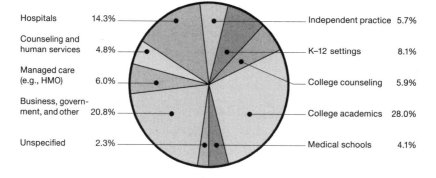

Hospitals 14.3%

Counseling and human services 4.8%

Managed care (e.g., HMO) 6.0%

Business, government, and other 20.8%

Unspecified 2.3%

Independent practice 5.7%

K–12 settings 8.1%

College counseling 5.9%

College academics 28.0%

Medical schools 4.1%

Where psychologists work
Source: Doctorate Employment Survey, APA Center for Workforce Studies, May 2011

You can't be good at or interested in everything.

The field of psychology may aim to understand everything about everyone, but it is a profession of specialties. A prospective psychologist should not expect to find every aspect of it appealing. Nor should a practicing psychologist seek to treat all prospective patients or present their methods as suited to everyone. Most people seeking psychological help would prefer to know that a prospective therapist has a specific approach that they can take or leave, rather than be told that the therapist's methods are adaptable to everyone.

A psychologist *can* be a generalist but must be prepared to refer clients to experts trained and experienced in the area of need.

98

distress
of an emotional
nature

disruption
in normal
functioning

deviance
from societal
norms

danger
to self or
others

The Four D's for determining if a patient has a disorder

A diagnosis is a judgment call.

Serious mental disorders often display symptoms that everyone experiences, such as sadness, confusion, anxiety, and demotivation. But there is no blood test that definitively indicates if such states represent normal emotions or severe clinical depression. Even psychiatrists diagnose patients predominantly on the basis of the patient's behavior, despite an intention to treat them physiologically. Further, a patient may exhibit symptoms of more than one condition, making any diagnosis a judgment call as to *whether* a label is applied and *which* label is applied.

Your struggles are rooted in your past. You must find the source, or you will undermine your future efforts.

Discovering the deep secret could take twenty years. And whether or not you find it, you will need new skills to move forward.

Psychodynamic therapy

Cognitive behavioral therapy

Seek a way *through,* not *out.*

Few problems brought into therapy can be solved outright. A therapist, rather than prescribe solutions that make difficult situations go away, helps patients deal with them. This may require the patient to examine earlier experiences, forgotten traumas, and ingrained behaviors that lead them to frame and respond to current situations unproductively, as well as to develop new skills to deploy in the future.

100

Nothing is truly broken; there is only the honoring of the journey.

Kintsugi, which translates to "golden joinery," is a 500-year-old Japanese tradition of repairing broken pottery. The artisan does not conceal damage but fills the cracks, chips, and voids with gold or silver. The fill may be smoothed to meet the original surface or raised above it.

In embracing imperfection, wear, and damage, *kintsugi* holds that an object has value not despite its flaws but because of them. Cracks are not permanent harms but are evidence of a deeper character brought about by having lived in the world. Highlighting rather than hiding flaws indicates that change and imperfections are not resented but are understood as new opportunities to make beauty.

Index

abnormality/deviance, 92, 95
abuse, 60, 93
actor-observer bias, 75
aggression, 33
agoraphobia, 27
alcoholism, 22, 27, 33
Alzheimer's disease, 22, 27
American Psychiatric
    Association, 37, 67
anger, 20, 38, 39, 63, 79, 85
animal behavior, 54, 55, 81
anorexia, 33
antisocial personality
    disorder, 33
anxiety/stress, 22, 33, 52, 53,
    57, 58, 64, 85, 86
apology, how to make, 45
Asch conformity
    experiments, 76
Asch, Solomon,
    psychologist, 76
attention deficit hyperactivity
    disorder, 27, 33, 92
autism, 22, 26, 27

Babyak, Michael, physician, 70
Barnum effect, 75
Barr, Sebastian Michael, 29

Beck's cognitive triad
    (negative triad), 50
behavior capturing, 54
bell curve, 9, 11
Bentall, Richard,
    psychologist, 50
Berne, Eric, psychiatrist, 41
bias, cognitive, 75
bias, in data, 7, 10
biological sex, 29
bipolar disorder, 27, 33
blind spot in eye, 73, 74
brain
    color, 16
    electrical activity in, 17
    injury, 19
    lobes, 16
    neurons/neurotransmitters,
        16, 17
    organization of, 19, 20, 21
    response to stimulus, 34
    vs. mind, 94
Bryan, Jennifer, 29
Buddha, 86
bystander effect, 78

Cahalan, Susannah, author, 89
cause-effect reversal, 62

Center for Gender Sanity, 29
character disorder, 42
Chicago Tribune, 4
childhood, development,
    24, 27
circumcision, 29
cognitive behavioral therapy,
    1, 100
cognitive bias/dissonance, 75
Columbo, Frank, television
    character, 88
communication, 38, 39, 41
conflict, interpersonal, 41
cortisol, 22

data/statistics
    application in practice, 96
    bias, 7, 10
    graphing, 2, 7, 9, 11
    mean/median/mode, 11
    narrative aspect of, 13, 14
    noise, 4, 7, 10
    presenting to audience, 14
    relevance in evaluating
        patients, 2, 96
    significance vs.
        importance, 12
decision-making, 57, 58

dendrites, 17
dependent personality
     disorder, 33
depression, 27, 33, 50, 70,
     85, 99
deviance/abnormality, 92, 95
Dewey, Thomas, U.S.
     presidential candidate, 4
diabetes, 22
diagnosis of mental illness,
     27, 35, 50, 67, 90, 91, 92,
     95, 99
*Diagnostic and Statistical
     Manual of Mental
     Disorders,* 37, 67, 78
Diamond, Jared, geographer
     and historian, 97
dopamine, 69
dreams, 79
drug dependence, 33
drugs/medication, 68, 69, 70,
     94, 95
Duchenne smile, 62
Dunning-Kruger effect, 49

earth, orbit of, 64
eating disorder, 27, 33
Ebbinghaus's forgetting
     curve, 47
Einstein, Albert, scientist,
     64, 65
emotions, physiology of, 31,
     32, 33, 38, 79
empathy, 26, 93, 95

endorphins, 69
Erikson, Erik, psychologist, 40
extroversion, 34
eye, 73

family, 28, 30, 40
Flaubert, Gustave, French
     novelist, 51
four D's for determining if a
     patient has a disorder, 99
Freud, Sigmund, neurologist,
     24, 79

Gage, Phineas, 19
gender, 29, 35, 36, 37
gene mutations, 22
generalized anxiety
     disorder, 33
Genovese, Kitty, 1964 murder
     of, 78
glands, hormone production
     in, 18
Global Positioning System
     (GPS), 64
Granville, Dr. J. Mortimer,
     inventor, 37
graphing of data, 2, 7, 9, 11
gray matter, 16
guilt vs. shame, 44

Hall, Calvin Jr., psychologist, 79
halo effect, 36
happiness, 32, 50, 51, 59
Hawthorne Study, 62

hindsight bias, 75
histrionic personality
     disorder, 35
hoarding, 27
Hobson, Allan,
     neuroscientist, 79
Holocaust, 28
hormones, 18, 22
Howes, Molly, psychologist, 45
humor, 36
hypertension, 22
hysteria, 37

impulse control, 33, 67
infants, 24, 28, 34
insanity, 67
intelligence, 49, 51
interquartile range (IQR), 11
introversion, 28, 34

Kintsugi, 101
Kohlberg, Lawrence,
     psychologist, 43

language
     brain regions associated
          with, 16, 20
     development, 24, 25
     as model of reality, 61
     vocabulary as indicator of
          intelligence, 84
Law of Parsimony, 15
Levinson, Richard, 88
Lewin, Kurt, psychologist, 47

life development
  adulthood, 27, 28, 34, 40,
    41, 43
  childhood, 24, 25, 26, 28,
    34, 43
  effects of childhood on
    adulthood, 60
  Erikson's life stages, 40
  moral development, 43
Lincoln, Abraham, U.S.
  president, 79
Link, William, 88
lying, 26

malingering, 90, 91
Maroney, McKayla,
  gymnast, 59
maximizers, vs. satisficers, 57
mean/median/mode, 11
medication/drugs, 68, 69, 70,
  94, 95
meditation, 66
medulla, 21
memory, 46, 47, 48
Menakem, Resmaa,
  psychotherapist, 30
mental illness, 1, 27, 50, 68,
  90, 91, 93, 94, 99
mental institutions, 89
mere exposure effect, 81
mind, vs. brain, 94
mitosis (cell division), 23
Money, John, expert in gender
  identity, 29
moral development, 43

motivation, 56
multiple personality
  disorder, 68
multiple sclerosis, 22

narcissism, 35, 42
nature vs. nurture, 1, 22, 23,
  29, 95
negative, definition, 8
nervous system, in various
  organisms, 20
neuron/neurotransmitter, 16,
  17, 18
neurosis, 42
noise, in data, 4, 7, 10

obsessive-compulsive
  disorder, 27
Olympics, 59
Oppenheimer, Daniel M.,
  psychologist, 84
orgasm, 37
oxytocin, 69

panic disorder, 27, 33
Parent-Adult-Child model, 41
parenting, 23
perception, visual, 71, 72, 73
personality, 28, 30
phobia, 27, 33, 81
Piaget, Jean, psychologist, 43
positive, definition, 8
post-traumatic stress disorder,
  33, 48
pregnancy, 22

problem-solving, 85, 86
procrastination, 85
projection, 87
Prozac, 69, 95
psychiatry, compared to
  psychology, 1
psychodynamic therapy, 1,
  100
psychology practice, 96, 98
psychopathy, 42
psychosis, 67
punishment, 8, 43

reading disability, 22
reality
  language as model of, 61
  perception of, 67
Reimer, Bruce/David, 29
representative sample, 2, 4, 11
research, see studies
reward/reinforcement, 8, 54,
  55, 56, 59
rheumatoid arthritis, 22
right and wrong, distinguishing,
  43, 44, 67, 76
Ritalin, 69
Rohn, Jim, author and
  motivational speaker, 77
Ronson, Jon, author, 91
Rosenhan, David,
  psychologist, 89
Rosenhan experiment, 89

satisficers, vs. maximizers, 57
schemas, 24

schizophrenia, 1, 8, 22, 26, 27, 33, 68, 68, 89
Schwartz, Barry, psychologist, 58
science, soft vs. hard, 96, 97
self-serving bias, 75
senses, transmission rates, 31
sensory gating mechanism, 68
serotonin, 69
sexual attraction, 31
shame, 44, 85
Skinner, B. F., behaviorist, 55
sleep, 18, 22, 79, 80
smiling, 62
social conformity, 76, 77
social development, 43
sociopathy, 42
soma, 17
spending money, 63
statistics, see data
studies/research
    application in practice, 96
    contradictions in, 62, 96
    papers, organization of, 82
    presenting, 13, 14, 15
    publication of, 78
    relevance in evaluating patients, 2, 96
    representative sample, 2, 4, 11
    subjectivity in, 7
    surveys, 4, 5, 6, 7, 12
    types, 3
    variables and controls, 3, 96
suffering, 85, 86
superstition, 55
surveys, 4, 5, 6, 7, 12
synapse development, 25
syphilis, 94
Szasz, Thomas, psychiatrist, 94

talking cure, 1
Tawwab, Nedra, mental health therapist, 39
teaching, how to, 83
terminal buttons, 17
theory of mind, 26
therapy, 1, 87, 88, 100
time, malleability of, 64, 65
transference, 87
trauma, 22, 28, 29, 30, 100
treatment of mental illness, 1, 70, 81, 95, 96, 99
Truman, Harry, U.S. president, 4
twins, 22, 23, 29

uterus/womb, 22, 23, 25, 37

Zajonc, Robert, social psychologist, 81
Zeigarnik, Bluma, psychologist, 47
Zoloft, 1, 70
zygomatic muscles, 62

Tim Bono, PhD, is a professor at Washington University in St. Louis and the author of *Happiness 101* and *When Likes Aren't Enough.* He has won several teaching awards and has been an expert consultant on psychological health and happiness for a number of national media outlets, including CNN, *Fast Company,* the Associated Press, and several public radio stations.

Matthew Frederick is a bestselling author, architect, urban designer, instructor of design and writing, and the creator of the 101 Things I Learned® series. He lives in the Boston area.